MARGARET WISE BROWN

Give Yourself to the Rain

poems for the very young

ILLUSTRATIONS BY TERI L. WEIDNER

FOREWORD BY LEONARD S. MARCUS

MARGARET K. McELDERRY BOOKS

New York London Toronto Sydney Singapore

For Adelaide and George Weidner
—T. W.

Margaret K. McElderry Books
An imprint of Simon & Schuster Children's Publishing Division
1230 Avenue of the Americas
New York, New York 10020

10 9 8 7 6 5 4 3 2 1

Library of Congress Cataloging-in-Publication Data

Brown, Margaret Wise, 1910-1952.
Give yourself to the rain and other poems / Margaret Wise Brown ; illustrations by Teri L.
Weidner ; with an introduction by Leonard S. Marcus.
p. cm.
ISBN 0-689-83344-X
1. Children's poetry, American. [1. American poetry.] I. Weidner, Teri L., ill. II. Title.

PS3503.R82184 G58 2001
811'.52—dc21
00-031023

MAY 0 8 2002

FIRST EDITION

foreword

During an intensely productive, fifteen-year-long career, Margaret Wise Brown (1910–1952) won acclaim as the author of *Goodnight Moon, The Runaway Bunny*, and more than one hundred other innovative illustrated books for the very young. Somehow during that remarkably brief span, Brown also managed to compose scores of lyric poems and nonsense rhymes, much of it meant for children. The twenty-four poems gathered in this varied collection are among the many left unpublished at the time of her sudden death, at the age of forty-two, of an embolism, while traveling in France. Published here for the first time, these poems give us the chance to enjoy a little-known side of the work of one of children's literature's best-loved authors.

What kind of poet was she? "To write well for children," Margaret Wise Brown once observed, "one must love . . . the things that children love." Brown wrote with a palpable feeling for nature—the great green room of sunlit fields, wild winds, silent woods, and the creatures that inhabit them. Believing that poetry for the young need not always be "light," she explored what she once called the "halftones" of the child's emotional experience—the sharp sting of loneliness and the shadowy hurt of feeling left behind. Brown also could be quite hilarious, as in this play-by-play of a crickets' quarrel: "Katy did—Katy didn't / Katy did—Katy didn't / Who cares!" She wrote in simple, repetitive forms that children might adapt for their own imaginative purposes.

A restless, dramatic, psychologically complex woman, Brown could work anywhere, scribbling poems on the backs of envelopes while stopped in New York traffic or out sailing, summers, off the Maine coast. A consummate craftsperson, she might fiddle with a single line for years, waiting patiently for the last word or syllable to fall into place.

Time and again, Brown's wide-eyed quickness of perception and seasoned dedication to craft come together in her poetry with satisfying force. Here, then, are poems that attest to the real magic to be gleaned from a loving attention to words and to the worlds within words, and within ourselves.

—Leonard S. Marcus

Leonard S. Marcus is the author of several exceptional books pertaining to children's literature, including *Margaret Wise Brown: Awakened by the Moon, Dear Genius: The Letters of Ursula Nordstrom,* and *Author Talk: Conversations with Judy Blume et al.* He lives with his family in Brooklyn, New York.

I Like Apples

I like apples
red apples
green apples
whole apples
half apples
ripe apples
rotten apples
crab apples
yellow apples
golden apples
glass apples
apple sauce, apple jelly

I like apples

Pussycat and the Pumpkin

Pusscatkin found a pumpkin.
He looked inside it.
Suddenly the pumpkin's eyes
Turned green and the pumpkin
Began to purr.
But where was
Pusscatkin?

The Monkey Man

The monkey man and his monkey
Are passing down the street
The monkey man and his monkey
Make music on the street.
It's happy turning music
That music on the street
It's turning dancing music
And it's in the monkey's feet.

In the Woods

Silence of the deep green wood
Where little sounds are heard
The flutter of such tiny wings
The buzz and sudden springs
Of grasshoppers flying from the grass
Where the shining beetle traffics pass
Near the roots of the long green grass

And in the birch trees

The rustling gust of sunlit leaves

The silence of logs, the coldness of stones

Deep in the deep green wood alone

Where the little sounds are heard

And the terrible clap of the wings of a bird

Flying to break

The high silence

Of the still blue sky.

Green Grass & Dandelions

Never has the grass been so green
Bright and green and growing
Never have the dandelions been so yellow
Bright yellow
Constellations
Brave little lions
Suns in the grass
Dandelions
In the green green green green grass
Never has the grass been so green
Bright and green and growing.
In any spring.

Give Yourself to the Rain

Give yourself to the rain when it falls
Give yourself to the wind
Go with it
Blow through the bright dark
Green light on trees
Listen to the rain
Again—through sleep
Dream of it
Brace nothing against it
Safe in your bed
Listen
And give yourself to the rain
When it falls down.

To a Boat Going over the Horizon

Go little boat

Go far from shore

Into the oceans

Mighty roar

Leave me here

On the empty shore

Where the great waves splash

And the seagulls soar

Go little boat

Forever more

Little Lost Kitten

Little lost kitten
Lost in the rain
I look for you
Over and over again.

Sun Came Out on a Summer's Day

The sun came out on a summer's day
And chased three little white clouds away
And shone on three trees near a deep blue pond
Where three little ducks were swimming around.

Near a house in a field
With a fence on a road
On the porch of the house
Sat a small tree toad
Looking down the road

And down the road
Came a truck with a load
Of hay
And a wild young horse
Who was running away
Out of the night
And into the day.

Boats

The boats on the river
Go puffing away,
Cutting the waters
They sail through the day.

With a chug and a puff
They pull their loads
Through the wet water
Without any roads.

Then they blow all their whistles
At the end of the day
And heading for home
They steam up the bay.

Pig Jig

Sing Big
  sing little
sing little
  Sing Big
A Great Big PIG
  and a little fat pig
Sing Big
  sing little
sing little
  Sing Big
Squeal Big
  squeal little
squeal little
  Squeal Big
Squeal like a PIG
  and a little fat pig
Jig Big
  jig little
jig little
  Jig Big
Jig like a big PIG
  dancing a jig

High on a Hill

High on a hill
When the moon is still
In the still night sky
A rabbit
Lifts his ears high
And listens
While the crickets fight
In the bright moonlight.
Katy did—Katy didn't
Katy did—Katy didn't
Who cares!
High on a high
When the moon is still
Up.

In the Sugar Egg

Deep in a round little bright little world
Deep in the Sugar Egg
A little horse was standing on one leg
In this Sugar Egg was a girl with a flower hat
And a dancing cat
In a world of wonderful secrets that
You can peep at.

The Sea-Slung Gong

Deep in the fog
A sea-slung gong
Sleepily rocks to its
Ding Dong Dong

Hark to the sound
Of the sea-slung gong
Ding Dong Dong
Ding Dong Dong

This is a warning
Not a song
Ding Dong
Ding Dong
Hark to the sound
Of the sea-slung gong

The Sound of the Wind Is a Wild Sound

The sound of the wind is a wild sound
It bristles the hairs on my back
The sound of the wind is the deep sound
Of all that I long for and lack

Christmas Song

O come little milk cows
O come to the barn
A baby is hungry
O do him no harm

O come little barn owls
O come to the barn
The wisest of babies
Is here keeping warm

O come all wild birds
Descend gentle dove
And all things from Heaven
To give him your love

O come little fishes
Flash out of the sea
A baby is smiling
On his mother's knee

O come little black sheep
O come right away
For all is forgiven
On this Christmas Day

There Is a Field Under the Sun

There is a field under the sun
Where a day's work is done
In ancient rhythms of soil,
Where sunset ends the day of toil
And one man against the sky
Bids the evening sun good-bye

Sleepy, Creepy Squirrel

Sleepy, creepy squirrel
Now remember me
Sleepy, creepy squirrel
climb up in your tree
Sleepy, creepy squirrel
Warm winds round your nest will curl
Soothe to sleep my sleepy squirrel
Sleepy, creepy squirrel
Now remember me

Colors

Shout Red Sing Blue Laugh Green
Smile Yellow Whoa Black

Red as a fire engine
Red as the fire
Red as a lobster
Red as a liar

Blue as the ocean
Blue as the sky
Blue as a bluebird
Flying by

Green as a shamrock
On Saint Patrick's Day
Green as a grasshopper
Jumping away

Yellow as a buttercup
Shining in the sun
Yellow as butter
On a toasted bun

Black as coal
Black as night
In the house of a mouse
Without any light

Red as roses
   Blue as the sky
      Green as the grass
         Black as a fly

The Big Boat Is Going to Sea

Toooot Toot
Toot Toot
The big boat is going
Out to sea
Past the big city
Out to sea

Look out little tug
Poky water bug
Look out flat ferry boats
Heavy come-and-go boats

Toot Toot
The big boat is going
Out to sea
The big boat is sailing away
Toooooot

Spring Madness

The red bird whistles in the tree
Spring is green
Endlessly
Endlessly
Ceaselessly
For an instant
In a tree.

Postman's Song

What will the postman bring today?
A letter from a sailor who has sailed away
A letter with a stamp from Mandalay
And a funny postcard from Casco Bay
Oh, what will the postman bring next week?

A letter from a man who's afraid to speak
Or a package of fish from Chesapeake
Oh, what will the postman bring next week?

For
What he'll bring you'll never know
The mail may be fast or the mail may be slow
The wind may blow, and the snow may snow
But the mail must go through

Through snow and rain and sleet and hail
Seven little postmen carry the mail
Through sleet and snow and dark of night
Put a stamp on your letter and seal it tight

Remember and Never Forget

Remember and never forget
Remember this
Your first snowstorm
White
And quiet in the night

And
Your first swim
The water was wet
And soft around you

And
The first hot day
When water came out of your skin
And rolled down you
You were so hot

Good-bye Little Bunny Good-bye

Good-bye little bunny Good-bye
You'll be a rabbit soon
And no one can catch you
Running away
Under the changing moon
Too soon
Good-bye little bunny good-bye
You'll be a rabbit
Soon

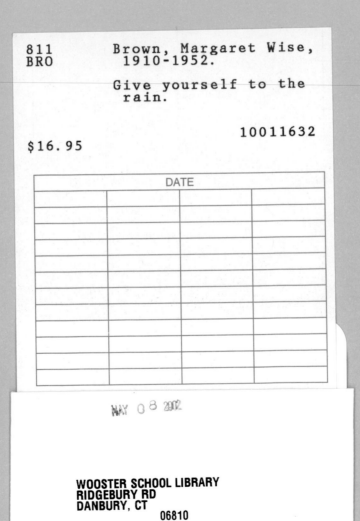